Mandala
Pretty Coloring Books

Copyright: Published in the United States by Janice Perrine
Published January 2017
ISBN-13: 978-1542640350
ISBN-10: 1542640350

Thank you

www.ingramcontent.com/pod-product-compliance
Lightning Source LLC
Chambersburg PA
CBHW081556280526
45788CB00011B/3483
9781542640350